Abroad With My Boys

in London and Paris

Summer 1978

by Donald B. Gibson

To Claire
from [signature]
Aug. 30, 2018

by Donald B. Gibson

For my sons David and Douglas
with loving memories of an unforgettable time!

Douglas, Donald, & David

INTRODUCTION

In the summer of 1978 I travelled with my sons, Douglas and David, on a brief and memorable end-of- summer vacation trip to London and Paris. Their mother did not accompany us. The travel plan was her idea. I agreed. The boys were eight and twelve years old. I was forty-five. The year was 1978. I can dredge up these dates because David was born in 1966 (which I can remember because his early kids' sports teams grouped the kids by the year they were born. David was always "66") and Douglas was born four years later in 1970. We planned the four years-thinking it would be better for everybody if the two of them were not in college at the same time.

I didn't know how long we were going to stay in either Paris or London. It didn't seem so important to know that in advance. We would go first to London; spend an undetermined length of time there; staying or leaving depending on what we might want to do at the time; then go to Paris to spend another undetermined length of time; then either return to London or return directly to the United States at some time or another, depending on how our money held out and other unknown and unknowable factors--such as whether we were having a really good time. We needed to return early enough to allow both boys to begin school on September 8th, the starting date that year for public schools in Princeton, NJ. No other time issues mattered much except that I had to get to my school (Rutgers University) to teach fall classes but not quite so early.

The boys' mother and I had separated a few months previous to this trip. Though I wasn't living with the boys during all the weeks leading up to this particular time, I lived in the same town and had previously lived with them all of their lives. Not only had I lived with them, I had participated actively in all phases of their upbringing from the very beginning. Their mother and I (especially she) had practiced the La Maze method of natural child birth with both children.

I knew a lot about domestic matters because when I was growing up in Kansas City, Missouri my mother (with my grandmother's and my siblings' help) cleaned our house at 2406 Brooklyn every Saturday that we lived there--top to bottom. Every room was swept and vacuumed, every surface was dusted, cleaned within an inch of its life. I also learned a lot about cooking, though I didn't learn to prepare meals until many years later. My mother taught each of my four sisters to prepare some part of a meal. But she didn't teach me or my brother that because, she said later on in life, that she did not want her black sons to become cooks in some white person's kitchen. I got to spend time in the kitchen, to watch my mother prepare food, to be with her, but not to learn to do what she was doing. In the third grade we learned fractions in part by following a recipe to bake cookies. My mother let me make cookies at home (following the school recipe and using fractions), but I was not encouraged to cook anything else (beyond toast and eggs).

I also learned grocery shopping. I was the youngest child and was very anxious to participate in the functioning of the household by going shopping with my mother. We didn't have a car then and the supermarket in the area of town (Kansas City, Mo.) where the poorest of us lived was rather far away. I walked those many blocks with my mother, quality time with her for me, the youngest child. None of my older siblings had the least interest in going with her. I loved it (grocery shopping) and do to this day.

So when I started living on my own in graduate school, I had some foundation on which to build my knowledge and understanding of food preparation.

Then there was my early experience with babies. My third sister had my nephew, Marc, "out of wedlock" ("wedlock" seemed like some royal designation to my twelve-year-old imagination). This event exposed me to another aspect of domestic life, caring for and feeding an infant. My sister and her child lived in my parents' house and I gladly and willingly learned just about all one needed to know about the care and feeding of a baby. I learned how to feed little Marc (sterilizing his bottles, dishes, and utensils); how to change (and wash) his diapers; bathe him and rock and sing him to sleep. I learned how to administer medications (knowledge, especially of folk remedies, readily and in quantity taught by my grandmother--my father's mother who lived with us much of the time). A job I had in college was caring during summer for the six-month-old child of one of my professors and his wife.)

So when JoAnne and I brought our babies home from the hospital, I knew a great deal about caring for them. I hope I handled that with awareness and sensitivity. She was young with a husband ten years her senior who happened to know more about babies and domestic affairs than she did. It did make it far easier for her to go to law school after our first child was four and the second a baby-- because I knew how to do everything to keep the household functioning.

I had been in my profession as a professor of English at a university long enough that during those years I could ease up a bit on my research, reading, and other professional responsibilities while she did what she needed to do to complete law school.

So by the time we proposed to the children that the three of us go to France and England I had spent a good deal of time with them. No strangers were we. I had no doubt about whether I could alone fill the parental needs they would have for a few weeks at ages eight and twelve. We had spent so much time together that they knew me very, very well and would have no difficulty whatsoever being with me and away from their mother for several weeks. My older son, unprompted, called me in his early years "da'-me" (daddy <u>and</u> mommy--combined) and his mother "ma'dee."- mommy <u>and</u> daddy combined)

We were going abroad because it seemed a very good proposal that their mother had made. We were heading for a divorce--not getting along very well. The children knew our lives were changing a lot when I moved out of the house to a one-room apartment closer to the center of town. Thereafter the boys would stay with me one night a week. I picked them up after school on Wednesdays, they would stay overnight with me; go to school on Thursday and return to their house after school on that day. I kept up with some school matters (making sure that homework was done when they were with me; going to parent/teacher conferences, making sure that they were supervised after school, though most days they were overseen by their mother's housekeeper). I sometimes took them to doctor's appointments and on occasion supervised after-school friends' visits to their place or mine.

At a certain point JoAnne proposed to me, not unreasonably, that I move back into the house because my older son at the age of fourteen needed the support and guidance of his father more so than that of his mother. She felt she did not know how to handle teenage male issues: shaving, bathing, dating, alcohol, sports. That made sense to me.

By the time we were about to leave on our trip abroad I had been back in the family house for several months and their mother had moved to an apartment. She suggested the trip abroad. The idea was to strengthen the bonds between the boys and me.

So at the end of July we boarded a helicopter at Newark International Airport and flew to JFK. Thereafter we transferred to Air India for London. An account of our journey follows.

WEEK I

Tuesday, July 25, 1978

Arrived in London this morning about 8:55. Had breakfast earlier on the plane at sunrise. By the time we had worked our way through customs it must have been 10 am. As we were leaving the airplane we heard announced that there was a message for "Mr. Gibson." "Oh, God," I thought, "What could it be?" Well, it was only a message from Air India telling me that my reservation was confirmed at the Arden House Hotel. It had two addresses: one Hugh St.; the other St. Georges' Drive. I inferred that there were two Arden house hotels. As we pulled into the British Airways Bus Terminal, I spotted a short distance away "The Arden House Hotel."

"That can't be it," I told myself. "That's too easy." I went inside the terminal and made my first British phone call and sure enough that hotel right up the street was the right one. Though it was only a short distance away, it was still something of a struggle to get our bags there since Douglas's bag was too heavy for him to manage easily. He struggled valiantly and we finally made it--with frequent stops--to the hotel.

We put our bags in our room after hearing from a very unpleasant Asian clerk that she could not understand how I could even conceive that children would pay a lesser amount for a room than adults since children take up as much space in bed as adults. I'm sure there must be other such clerks; I just never met them. She certainly

10

didn't believe me when I said (ugly-American-like) in "American hotels children are often free." So the 18 pds. per night figure was a correct one. I determined to spend at least the first night there and perhaps one more before looking for something less expensive. At thirty-six dollars a day for room and breakfast alone I found our expenses for the first day to amount to fifty dollars and at that rate we could do relatively little else. That simply would not do!

We decided to go for a walk to get maps to determine where we were and what was around us. We finally discovered that what I had thought was Victoria Station was in fact Victoria COACH Station. After our walk and a brief nap we decided to take a walk to Buckingham Palace. Just as we got there Douglas suddenly felt sick (I think he was tired and hungry after our long trip and the little sleep we had had.) He leaned against a fence and said he felt he was going to throw up. I suggested we sit on the grass in front of the Palace. Just as Douglas decided he had had enough sight seeing, and that he was ready to return to the hotel, I saw a guard resplendent in his red uniform.

We decided to cross over and have a closer look. We watched for a while and Douglas's spirits began to perk up a bit. Then, to our surprise and delight, we suddenly saw a whole array of guards, and we just happened to be there when the change was about to take place. We watched the entire procedure. During the course of it I felt a wet splat on my forehead. I turned to David and asked whether what I thought was on my forehead was indeed there.

"Yes," he said. "That's what it is."

"Hm," I thought. "I wonder what that means? Is it that all this pomp and circumstance doesn't amount to a pile of . . .?" I fortunately had a wad of Kleenex in my pocket and was able to clean up a bit.

Donald B. Gibson

The Boys and Buckingham Palace

We left Buckingham Palace and walked a short way to a tiny restaurant on Palace Road. David and Douglas ordered beef burgers and I ordered stuffed heart. We could hardly contain ourselves when the burgers came. There were two on each plate with "chips" and tomatoes. The beef burgers were about a quarter of an inch thick; no, the width of a half dollar, and difficult to cut with a knife. My heart with rice and peas was quite tender and delicious. I think it was a lamb heart. We then went back to the hotel and had a nap. I suspect it was about three or so. We slept until 5:30 and all of us had the feeling we had slept through the night. Douglas insisted we should have

12

breakfast; David wasn't sure what day it was; and I felt as though I was in the middle of a ninety-six hour day.

We decided to go out again and simply on a whim jumped on a double-decker bus and rode to the end of the line and back. In doing that we saw parts of London we would not otherwise have seen. The whole trip took about three hours or so and David and Douglas were delighted with such a long ride on the top of the huge bus in the very front of the upper deck.

When we returned we went looking for a place to eat and ended up eating cheeseburgers at Wimpy's. These were much better than their burgers at the Palace Road restaurant. But they were not better than my lamb heart, not by a long shot. Then we went home and went to bed. Thus ended the longest day of my life (seemingly) and our first day in London.

WEDNESDAY. July 26

We got up today a little before eight (we have to be at breakfast between eight and nine), showered and went to have our first English breakfast. We had toast, orange juice, an egg and bacon. It was not bad, but it was different from what we were used to. The bacon was quite lean but not crisp--limp and seemingly more boiled than fried. The egg was very greasy and I couldn't imagine how it had been cooked.

We sat with a young Irishman who was working at something (I don't recall what) in London. He seemed to be interested in people who had yearnings to do unusual things, people who were rather single-minded about what is important in life. He talked about the "flat earth society" and their thoughts and inclinations. He spoke of a group that plans to raise the Titanic. Our sharing a table has been a not-unusual occurrence this little time since we've been here. Sharing a table with strangers is not unheard of in restaurants in the U.S., but it is not a common nor usual practice. That has something to do with its inhabitants' sense of space in the U.S. Spaces in restaurants in the U.S. are larger; the amount of space that there generally is devoted to restaurants in the country as a whole is much greater than in Europe. In general living spaces are larger in the U.S. than in Europe. I think that's true. I 've believed it forever.

After breakfast we went out to see if we could do something about our obviously untenable monetary situation. I had by this time begun to feel very, very anxious. At fifty dollars a day we weren't going to make it to the 15th of August--to say nothing of the 3rd of September. I felt extremely anxious about a variety of things, a state I tried not to communicate to the children because their being upset would do nothing good for anybody. I first called AIR INDIA to check on our return. "You can't possibly get a return flight before the 10th of September," the agent pronounced. My heart fluttered and dropped (or so it seemed). "But I've already requested a reservation for the week of August 23rd or September 3rd." He checked his records and told me I was down for the week of September 3rd. That was a considerable relief. Then I turned to face the immediate housing situation.

I finally found a place that rents flats called, appropriately enough, "Flat Lands." I spent two hours in there and in the two hours the maximum amount of money I could spend per week grew from thirty pounds to forty-five. We finally left the agency and took our first "tube ride" to Earls Court Station where we were to meet Mr. Clark and see the flat he had for rent.

We finally got there and Mr. Clark led us up to the third floor--to a garret with a hot plate, three narrow beds, three plates, three cups, three knives, three forks and two spoons. "It's going to be tough having company for dinner," I said to Mr. Clark. He was not amused.

I said almost immediately--I think I blurted it, "We'll take it!" We returned to Victoria Station and adjourned to Wimpy's for lunch. I vowed that was the last Wimpy's meal that my poor children were going to eat in London. Then went home and I began to worry that Mr. Clark was going to keep my 90 pounds and swear he'd never seen us before (Even though I had a receipt.) Then I began to worry whether the place had lice or bed bugs or both. I told David and Douglas to be quiet for a while because I needed to meditate. Thank God (or more specifically, Pat Carrington, a therapist in Princeton) for teaching me meditation.

After thirty minutes I had my whole situation in far better perspective, realizing that the worst thing likely to happen is that I would spend time and money getting back home early. Still I am not certain that we can afford Paris since it is going to cost at least three hundred dollars just to get there and back. We will see.

We all had a nap, then went for a ride on a double decker, this time in a northerly direction and through Piccadilly Circus. We've asked many people for directions as we move about London and people have without fail been most kind and helpful. The Brits I have so far met have been a wonderfully warm people. I'm sure there are some evil characters out there but I haven't met them, not yet anyway.

We returned from our ride alighting at Victoria Station. This time I determined we were not going to eat at Wimpy's. Instead we went to the Station Cafeteria and the food we had there made Wimpy's look like ultra-fine dining. We walked home, bought some postcards on the way, wrote a few home (which we have yet to mail), played Scrabble, and went to bed. I could not sleep finding new things to worry about regarding the flat, getting there tomorrow, etc.

David and Douglas nearly drove me crazy with their bickering all evening. They probably sensed my own worry and discomfort. I'm fine after I get to meditate a bit. Thus ended our second day in London.

THURSDAY, JULY 27--

Today is our moving day. We got up before eight, dressed and had our last breakfast at Arden House. There was an American couple there from Georgia, and she found her egg too soft. Her husband, meaning to convey the idea that the cook should put the egg back in the pan and turn it onto its softer side and let it cook a bit more said over and over, "just tu'n it ov'a.; just tu'n it ov'a." His accent was so heavy that we would not have known what he was saying if we had not understood his Southern accent and known the subject of the discourse. It struck us as extraordinarily comical that no one at Arden House seemed to have the slightest idea what he was saying. From then on til the end of our trip Douglas or David would break us up simply by saying, "tu'n it ova; tu'n it ova."

Breakfast finished, we went to our room, packed, and stacked our bags outside the hotel. Two taxi drivers refused to take us to our new place: " Sorry, Guvnor," one said. "I'm just on my way to breakfast." "Sorry, mate," said the other, "that's just in the wrong direction."

We finally carried the bags to Victoria Coach Station. I figured that if I simply approached the lead taxi there, he couldn't refuse. He didn't refuse. We finally got to our new quarters. I rushed upstairs, pulled back the bed clothes and didn't see a single bed bug. I looked for roaches too, but saw no sign of any such creature.

We settled in then went out to explore the neighborhood. My archenemy, Wimpy (of burger fame) was just around the corner. Worse yet, Ronald McDonald was only a   block away. So far we've managed largely to avoid them.

This is truly a mixed neighborhood. People here are from everywhere. Caribbeans, Africans, Asians. Europeans of every variety. When the taxi driver let us out he (a European of some stripe, I suppose) said: "Oh, I don't like these people here. All Arabs! I just don't like them!"

"Oh," I said, "I'll get along alright." "Well, good luck," he said. "I just don't like them!"

That afternoon we decided to go to Madame Tussaud's wax museum. I was learning that any trip with D&D has a far more likely chance of success if they are in on the major aspects of planning such as choosing the destination. There was a long queue and I thought it would take us hours to get in. As it was, the wait was only about forty-five minutes or so. We had to pay constant close attention because it was not always so easy to tell who was wax and who was flesh and bone. I almost took a photo of a tourist who was resting on a couch looking very wax, but apparently quite real. An employee or a wax figure? I'm not totally sure. "He's a fake, Dad." Douglas whispered. "I can just tell it." People were examining this figure quite closely.

I took a photo of David and Douglas standing next to Lenin and Mao Tse Tung. I hope they come out. David was disappointed because he didn't have flash bulbs and was unsure whether there was light enough for his photos. We saw famous American and English figures, mostly political figures or royalty. Lots of British murderers who had done away with many of their fellow citizens.

We had a picnic lunch with us (bread and cheese--I must get these children some fresh fruit) but we decided (for whatever reason) to go home and eat it there. Dave and Doug spent the rest of the afternoon playing with cars and airplanes they had bought at a shop down the street. I took a long nap. Later we again explored the neighborhood and discovered the best place to eat so far, the New Hot Pot on Earl's Court Drive. We had dinner: Dave, spaghetti; Doug, baked chicken, and I, kidneys. Finally decent meals--even though they won't eat the peas. No feeding by force though they refuse to eat the peas. ("Good to have something you can refuse to do; practice for when the Nazis come, I warn them.)

We returned home--D.& D. to play with their cars and I to begin writing in my journal. We stayed up late--I jittery again about what we are going to do about our money disappearing so fast. I slept fitfully--as I usually do in a new place--and I didn't get bitten by a single bed bug--because there aren't any here! I'm going to compete for the Guinness medal for World Worriers. I'll be the western world's chief contender.

FRIDAY, JULY 28

We slept late this morning--Doug 'til about 10, David 'til 10:40, and I until 11. I had decided to do laundry this morning but put it off 'til-- well, we'll see when I put it off to. We had breakfast--cheese, bread, tea, orange juice and a multiple vitamin over lightly. David and Doug played with their cars again. They are delighted with them because they are so well designed and sturdy--well, that may be part of the reason. They decided they needed two more vehicles. We got out about 12:30, bought the cars at the nearby shop, went to the post office and set out for the Imperial War Museum.

David was disappointed because he couldn't take photos inside without flash bulbs. I was disappointed because I had left my camera at home in the U.S. Douglas was bored as he frequently was and said he didn't feel well. We decided to eat lunch on the grounds of the museum. We did that and decided to return to the Imperial War Museum when we had our cameras (at least those of us who COULD have our cameras.) Then we thought about going to Westminster.

We worked up our courage to take the Underground or "Tube" as the subway is known. When we got off we were confused. Where were we? A man saw us looking at signs--a well-dressed, middle-class citizen who only meant well. "Where are you going?" he asked.

I really didn't feel that we needed his help. But he wanted to help us, and I felt it was my duty to allow him to do that, insofar as it would not be too great a hindrance to the furtherance of our ends.

"Westminster" I said. "Come along," he said. But then, upon looking at a map, it looked as though we were already at Westminster.

"Oh," our benefactor said. It looks as though we're already there. They've changed the name."

"Thank you," I said as he jumped on his train having finished "helping" us.

"He's wrong," Dave said. We should have gotten back on the subway and gone another stop." Of course David was right.

We finally got to Westminster, saw the Houses of Parliament, Big Ben, and Westminster Bridge. We walked across the bridge and sat for a long while by the Thames on the Queen's Walk. The day cooled a bit and it was very, very pleasant to sit there. Whenever the kids would see a pigeon, they'd say, "Look out, Dad!"

The weather was just marvelous, as it almost always has been since we've been here. One morning was a bit drizzly, but that soon cleared up. The days have been sunshiny-bright and just cool enough to be really comfortable--about 70 or 72 degrees at mid-day.

We made our way leisurely back to our neighborhood, Earl's Court, and had dinner again at The New Hot Pot. Again we paid less than three pounds for a really good dinner for the three of us. I have become such a tightwad that I've almost given up alcohol--had only two beers since we've been here. I had two Shandies with dinner but they cost only 20p. each. Again I've spent a good part of the day thinking about money and how we're going to make it through our time here, especially if we go to Paris as I would so love to do. It appears that if we don't go to Paris and we spend no more than six pounds per day beyond housing for the next forty days, we can do it.

But it was obvious to me after today that that is no way to live. So I wrote to JoAnne and told her we were coming home after the middle of August. I feel so much better now. I'll just have to see what I can work out with the airlines. We spend at least 3 pounds for our supper and a pound and a half on the tube. That leaves a pound and a half for breakfast and all else. This is no way to spend a vacation. David and Douglas were both very disappointed when I said we would not be going to France. But they quickly reconciled themselves to the fact and have accepted it gallantly.

In the evening after supper, David was reading this journal to us. When David got to the bottom of the page, Douglas said "Tu'n it ovah; just tu'n it ovah." We all found that hilarious.

But even with that I didn't sleep well. Wonder why?

SATURDAY, JULY 29

Up this morning about 9:30. Laundry day. Tried time after time to call Air India. No luck. Bought raspberry jam, apples and cheese for breakfast. The kids have been great at adapting to eating whatever I provide for breakfast. Not once have they asked for anything other than what I set before them. They got involved in playing with their cars while I gathered up our laundry. I can't believe that I was so dumb as to plan to do laundry on a Saturday morning, the same time that ninety percent of the inhabitants of London would decide to go to the laundromat. We sat there for a while before I declared next Monday national washday.

We returned home from the laundromat and had lunch. David and Douglas got involved in a game they invented called "pence hockey" while I napped.

My rest is not helped by the fact that we hear the underground trains from below our windows. Thankfully its fully four stories below and no closer. That helps. We had decided earlier to go see HMS Discovery near Temple Station. Dave woke me at three and we set out. (These many years later I cannot understand why we would have wanted to leave so very, very early.) Douglas was not too keen on going, but finally he relented. I can't imagine what we would have done had Douglas not relented. No way would I have left him alone in our flat!

We saw the Discovery tied up on the Thames on Victoria Embankment near Waterloo Bridge. We then walked leisurely along the Thames all the way to Westminster Bridge and to Parliament Square where we took photos and watched people. We had fun setting the camera on a wall, focusing it and taking our own picture after I set the timed shutter release and knelt between D. and D. before the shutter snapped. One such photo appears toward the beginning of this book. We took the underground back home.

When we came to Earl's Court Road, I asked David where was the bag that had the cameras in it. Alas! He had left it on the subway!! He was filled with remorse. He said he wouldn't go out with us to dinner; he was only going to have bread and water. He cried and felt "just terrible." We at last convinced him at least to come with us to eat. As time passed, he eventually felt better and finally consented to eat. (I think he's recovered since after a fairly full dinner he is now eating bread and jam.). We did less well than we've done on our economy effort, spending over three pounds and not our usual 2.75 pounds or less.

Monday we will call Lost and Found and see if some honest soul has found our cameras. And I think about getting some ink to encourage the boys to practice their penmanship. And mine, come to think about it.

This marvelous weather has turned hot. It is not nearly as comfortable as it was earlier in the week, but at least it isn't raining

I"ll try calling Air India tomorrow.

SUNDAY, JULY 30

I tried Air India for half an hour without success. Will try again tomorrow.

Today is a rainy day. We all really need a rest. Douglas is homesick and wants to go home. As far as he is concerned we could go home tomorrow. Or so he says. This too will change. I hope.

I went out this morning to mail letters, get bread, and be by myself for a short while. David and Douglas again are at each other. All day (seemingly) at home or away. Douglas seems constantly needful of provoking response. He is now saying he is angry with me and deciding he is going to sleep in the bed furthest away. (Which is really kind of sweet.)

They have been playing games all day and seem not to mind this day of rest from outside activity. I took a long nap this afternoon. I seem so tired everyday. I suppose I am under more stress than I realize.

I went out to buy ink today so I could practice my penmanship. It's coming along quite well. Inspired by my example D. and D. tried it too. For Douglas it turned out to be somewhat frustrating and not so rewarding. For David (of course, because he's older) it was a far more successful undertaking. He worked at it for a long time

We had a good dinner tonight at the New Hot Pot. I had steak and mushroom casserole; D and D had chicken a la king. We are limiting ourselves to one pound each for dinner and for that amount we can get a very filling dinner--including dessert. This has not been the best of days, but I am sure I will feel better when I know how long we are going to be here and what our budget must be.

David beat me at scrabble last night for the very first time. I think the score was 255 to 239.

The sky is awfully dark outside. I hope the weather will be better tomorrow.

WEEK TWO

MONDAY, JULY 31

A dark and dreary day. Raining hard. I decided to take laundry to laundromat again. Crowded!!! Brought it back home for the second time. Caretaker Gordon of our flat says I should take it up and leave it with the operator. She will wash it and it costs very little more than it would otherwise. I did that later, leaving the kids happily playing various automobile games and dropping our laundry off at the laundromat. My "waterproof" raincoat is not waterproof after all.

We decided to spend the day inside. They don't seem to mind at all not going out. Douglas spent hours practicing Italic script and being very proud that he could make the letters so well. I was proud of him too that he had stuck with it until he could make very beautiful letters.

I Finally got through to Air India. "I would like to return to U.S. on the 17th of August."

"Well," the agent said, "there will be a fine of $50."

"That's not so bad," I thought.

"And then you'll have to pay a full fare--an additional $207 per ticket."

"We're staying," I said to myself. "I don't know how we're going to do it but we are."

I meditated for a LONG time and afterwards felt confident that it could be done. I also saw a sign today advertising a Paris excursion for 14 pounds. If that excursion is available, perhaps we can go to Paris if only for a few days--perhaps a week or so. I'll have to look into it.

I did some reading this afternoon. The day went fast. We went out for dinner about 6:30. Had a good and satisfying meal. We are going to look for another good restaurant tomorrow on Hogarth St. Ours is good, but some variety would be welcomed. Frommer says there are decent, inexpensive restaurants on Hogarth. We played scrabble last night. Will go to the Underground's "Lost and Found" to see if our bag of cameras has shown up.

TUESDAY AUGUST 1

I suppose I'll have to accept the fact that D& D do not want to sight-see everyday. We seem to have fallen into a pattern. We get up in the morning and the boys play one of several games. We have breakfast. They get dressed and play more. I straighten up--they wash breakfast dishes and put away food. We almost never get out before noon or one. We decide to do one or two things (to go one or two places) from one o'clock to five-thirty. We come back. They play until 6:30. We go out to dinner and return about 7:30. They play. I read or write in my journal. We usually play scrabble until 10:30 or 11:00. After putting on jammies Douglas falls asleep during the game and is the first one up in the morning.

The weather was mostly cloudy today but dry and cool--though not cool enough for a jacket. We decided to do two things: to go to Baker Street Station to the Underground Lost and Found and from there to the British Museum. We went to Baker Street and of course the bag with the cameras in it was not there. We were told to return on Thursday or Friday. I certainly don't expect to see that bag in life again. Douglas had a stomach ache by the time we reached Russell Square. Lunch seemed to take care of of his stomach ache. We proceeded to the Museum. In front of the Museum was a 1965 Volvo sedan exactly like the one I bought in that very year in Copenhagen. But that's another story too long to tell here. It was gorgeous and in mint condition.

We went into the museum and Douglas wanted at once to sit down. Then he wanted to come back to our apartment because he was bored! "Why didn't you leave me at home in Princeton?" he asked. "I didn't want to come here in the first place."

I was quite moved to see manuscripts penned by Samuel Johnson, Boswell, Keats, Shelly, Byron, Wordsworth, etc. Too much to take in all at once. I didn't think we should stay so very long if Douglas were ever to have a chance to appreciate the place, even to like it a little bit. (What I fear here is the possibility that Douglas might react negatively and hate it forever if anyone were to try to force the place on him. Better to bring him back when he's older. David seemed open to it. He seemed to look forward to coming again when we would have more time.

We left the museum and sat again on benches at Russell Square. The boys examined my new beard (which I am growing, by the way, because the outlets here won't accommodate my razor and I don't want to shave with a safety razor) and commented generally about my facial hair. Douglas had an ice cream - a good cure for stomach aches. We returned home --David unerringly guiding us each step of the way.

We went to a new restaurant on Hogarth St., the Hot Pot. The food was very much like that at the New Hot Pot--prices about the same. I suspect the two places must use the same kitchen, surely the same cook. We returned home.

Douglas has been very disappointed because he wants a particular toy car. David was going to buy it for him but discovered it would have taken all of his money. I think Doug is less disappointed now since David has promised to sell him his car when they get back home. They are now examining my camera. (There is a mystery here for me. I don't know what camera this is that I refer to. The present moment is Thursday February 15, 2018. I was under the impression that I had left my own camera (a Russian camera I had bought in Poland in the early 60's) at home in Princeton, NJ. I don't know what accounts for its being here at this moment in time.)

More games. I am utterly amazed at the invention exhibited by these children in contriving games; utterly amazing. They can keep themselves busy for hours and hours on end. Played scrabble. Doug got angry because he insisted on adding up the total score at each turn and it was taking far too long. He quit playing in the first round and fell off to sleep. His whole problem was that he was very tired. We played until around 11pm. At 11:30 an obnoxious neighbor came home and started playing loud music. I slammed some doors in protest and so did other occupants. He persisted until about midnight.

WEDNESDAY, AUGUST 2

Rainy, rainy day. The boys were up early, Douglas first, and they at once began their games. They have what seems to be 95 vehicles (surely I exaggerate) bought with the money their grandfather gave them before they left home. They go on secret missions, protecting the world from such villains as "Gold Butt," the mad monster who has a screw in his navel holding his golden butt (or so they say) in place and who is bent on extracting the world's last dime from it. They have undiscoverable hideouts and utterly invincible weapons. The children never run out of ideas.

I went out for bread, Irish Cheddar, Dutch Gouda, and pineapple juice. I also bought The London Times. Breakfast, then back to the game. We decide to spend the day inside. It is raining fiercely and I find that things go best if I adjust my own pace to theirs. They simply do not want to sight-see all day every day, and I have decided not to press them. We have a long time here and if we spend three to five hours daily seeing things we will have seen a lot by the time we're done.

By this point I have decided that we will indeed be here until the week of September 4th. France seems to be out of the question--we can't afford the cost unless we scrimp more than I am willing to. After we pay our 45 pounds per week rent we can make it if we average 7 to 8 pounds per day on all other expenses. The boys are quickly adjusting to our budget and even seem to enjoy participating in staying with it.

Douglas is in a wretched mood today. Nothing is right. He is as angry with me as a nest of invaded hornets and has been arguing with David all day. He seems a little better after I make a punching bag out of a pillow and blankets and encourage him to punch them as long and as hard as he wants. I later discovered (surprise, surprise!) he is sleepy too. He got up very early this morning and went to bed relatively late last night. His phrases for the day:"Don't come near me, Dad" or "See! that (whatever "that" is) proves you like David more than me!"

Still the day passes fast and we have a good dinner at the New Hot Pot, still our favorite place. I wrote cards and letters, wrote in my journal, read a bit, meditated and napped. Scrabble and all to bed by 9:30.

THURSDAY, AUGUST 3

Again we awaken to a downpour. We have breakfast and then the games begin. I go out shopping--mostly for lunch. I also decided to buy a padlock since I had a fantasy last night about walking in and finding all of our belongings gone. I noticed that all the doors have hasps and many people put locks on when they go out. I reason that they must know something that I don't. So if we are ripped off--it won't be because I neglected to buy a padlock.

What a honey-tempered boy Douglas is today. So loving, cooperative. Not once today has he said, "I want to go home." He hasn't started a single fight.

The day cleared up a bit by noon or so and we went to the British Museum of Natural History. A very fine afternoon. Lots of very interesting things to see including a super exhibition showing how the human body works. It would take a full day to go through the whole exhibition carefully. Douglas very much enjoyed the birds and the insects. We have two more trips yet to do there--the Science Museum and the Victoria and Albert Museum.

The caretaker of the building where we are staying is a young man named Mr. Clarke. He is very funny--a bit effeminate and he utterly detests the tenants (I suspect that includes me). He has put up signs all over saying what the nasty tenants have done and how they should correct their habits. Example: "Would the person responsible for putting newspaper in the toilet please refrain from that unhygienic and nasty practice. Toilet paper is available from the caretaker by request."

He told me today in utter disgust how someone on the second floor had urinated and fornicated on a sheet and then thrown it in the trash. At the same time he is a most casual caretaker. The window sash in our room is about to fall off--any day now. There is dust and grime all over. The shower curtain is a rag, and rain falls through the skylight above the stairway. He has his hours posted on his door and sternly warns against bothering him for any reason other than the most dire emergency--that means, I gather, nothing short of fire.

The people in this area of London are very diverse in terms of ethnic and racial origin. The Arabs and the Middle Easterners here are not guest workers and are by no means poor. If there are any here that appear not well-off, I have not seen them. Many have autos and their children appear to be dressed well. Many of the women follow tradition and go about veiled--only the veils that I see appear to my untutored eye like Holloween masks. Others dress in modern fashion, some rather ordinarily, others in high fashion. It is interesting to see men flirting with modern women. They lean very close to them as the women pass on the street and seem to whisper something. The women--at least those I have seen--simply keep walking as though they have heard nothing. Many of the men wear suits of good cut and fine cloth; others wear traditional garb. Some dress in a very ordinary fashion--sweaters and trousers. The shop owners I see appear to be Indians and Pakistanis. I'm not really sure. I've never seen such an admixture of people of mixed and varied races; people of all hues, hair textures, features.

We go out to dinner about 6:15. I buy two cheap thrillers and read for most of the evening. I don't often find it easy to grab a few moments to myself.

FRIDAY, AUGUST 4

Our usual morning--nothing new. About noon we decide to go out after we've had lunch. Today is the day we go to Lost and Found to see if the bag with the two cameras has been turned in from the subway. We have been speculating since we lost them--and especially since our trip there last Tuesday. Are we going to get them back? Is there any chance we will get them back. Douglas claims to be neutral, but every day he insists we look at new cameras, price them, and then he worries me to spell out the circumstances under which they will get new cameras and when that time will be as well.

So by the time we got to Lost and Found we were not very hopeful. Our lost cameras cost $25-$30 and even more here in England. What were the chances that someone would have found them and turned them in? We stood in line and waited without much hope. Our turn came. The clerk asked us to describe the bag and she asked whether there was a name inside it. We showed her the twin bag that we carried with us; a bag that looked EXACTLY like the bag we'd lost; a bag that had a large likeness imprinted on it of "The Jolly Green Giant;" and below a likeness of the giant, saying: "Ho, Ho, Ho."

She then asked whether one of our names was in the bag?. Then the brands of the cameras. "I think we've got it," she said. (What more evidence could she have possibly wanted?) Finally she produced the bag.

David especially expressed incredible relief. He had felt total responsibility for the bag's loss. But we all were greatly, greatly relieved. Did we learn anything about the nature of humankind? Did I point a moral? If I didn't, I certainly am glad I didn't. Would this have happened in the U.S.? Would we have gotten the bag back? Maybe. Possibly. Who knows? We were high all evening and so very happy

That evening Douglas asked me to tuck him in and sing him a song. "What shall I sing?"I asked. I think he was asking for some touch with the past and the familiar. On second thought I don't think I know WHY he asked for that particular song. I had sung it to him a time or two but it was certainly not a thing I did habitually or often.

Sing "The Black Anthony?"

"The what??" I asked.

"The "Black Anthony," he said.

"You mean 'The Black National Anthem?'"

"Yes, that."

Why did it occur to him to ask for that particular song? Why did he even remember it? And why did he remember it in that way? I'm sure I'll never figure that out. Especially since I can't imagine what the song could <u>possibly</u> have meant to him. It meant something of importance, though. I'm inclined to ask him when I next see him. But I probably won't. He's in his 40's now.

SATURDAY, AUGUST 5.

David and Douglas at the London Zoo

Originally we had decided to go to Greenwich by boat, but we want a really good day to do that and today the weather is rather uncertain. We decided instead to go to the zoo. We had a very pleasant walk from the Baker Street. Station, through Regents Park to the zoo. Regents Park is very beautiful and well taken care of. A stunning rose garden and flowers of many different varieties. We had a great afternoon roaming about the zoo...lions, tigers, and elephants--lots of birds. I had forgotten how much fun zoos are to visit with kids.

At the end of three and a half hours we were ready to go home. We had to ask directions to the right train--something we haven't had to do for a long time. We had a somewhat late dinner. Home. Scrabble. To bed. Sometime today I finished my detective story and started a new one. They cost about 20 cents each and are well worth it.

SUNDAY, AUGUST 6TH

The kids decided they didn't want to go anywhere today. I gave them 1 pound each for the week and we went to WH South on Earl's Court Road, primarily a book store. We bought books--or the kids did--and spent practically the whole day reading. I meditated and napped for about an hour. Went out with Douglas to pick up laundry. Discovered tonight that they had not dried Douglas's blanket well. He'll sleep under bed spreads and I'll leave the windows up only a tiny bit.

A little sun today but mostly cloudy. You can never tell when it is going to rain. It finally did just as we got into a new Hotpot Restaurant we found on Kenway Road, not far away. The elements were gracious enough to desist by the time we finished and made our way out. Since those first days when the weather was so marvelous it has been mostly cloudy all the time. It usually manages to rain at least once every twenty-four hours.

We've all been reading all evening. No Scrabble tonight. The streets are so quiet now that either it is raining or the country has run out of booze. Douglas is the picture of   calm and innocence as he sleeps next to where I am writing. Such a sweet child!
So lucky to have them both.

When we first came it seemed as though the days passed so very slowly. Now they are going faster and faster, and I know that all too soon I am going to look up and it will be time for us to return home! Already I am dreading that moment. I'm even growing fond of this grundgy old room.

I finally understand why painters don't come to England to paint. The light in the country is never the same for fifteen minutes at a time. The sky changes constantly throughout the day. I've never been in a place with such weather. (Homemade myth.)

What a lazy waste of a day this was. Its total worthless quality was objectified by our going to McDonald's for dinner. We read all day; the kids didn't get their clothes on 'til five o'clock. I vow to have no more days like this. It did rain a good part of the day but we didn't even go out for a walk between showers (which we could have managed).

Tomorrow has got to be better!

WEEK THREE

MONDAY, AUGUST 7

And a good day today certainly was! We got up fairly late (8:30) and had our usual breakfast--pita, strawberry jam, Dutch gouda, orange juice and tea. D &D messed around a bit, destroying the room as they do in their play every day. By ten o'clock I called a halt--told them to dress and prepare to go out. They were great. They not only put on their clothes, but they insisted that I sit down and pretend that I weren't there while they cleaned up--picked up everything, made the beds, washed the dishes and put our bags away in the wardrobe in order to make the room neater. After they finished, David said: "Guess we won't need Mrs. Macklin [their mother's housekeeper] anymore." We headed out to the British Museum of Science.

The Museum is perfectly incredible. We got there about 11:30 and by five o'clock we had gone through the third floor and half the fourth. It is so engaging and there is so much that I cannot begin to recount our total experience.

The kids were thoroughly engaged in the history of aviation. We spent a really long time there. A section on temperature and the measurement of temperature got great attention. There were irresistible sections on computers, nuclear fission, the history of radio, television, telephone. Many of the sections had working exhibits. A lot of the exhibited pieces are very, very old and their histories are traced quite vividly and clearly, We were in the physics section when we quit, and I guess we'll start in there tomorrow. I figure we should finish this museum by Thursday. (Two more days.) Then we will have to do the Museum of Geology, and then that will leave the Albert and Victoria Museum--God knows how long that will take. And besides their being extra-ordinarily interesting, they are free!

We paused for lunch about two o'clock. We went outside to eat our bread, cheese, plums and soda. It stopped raining momentarily, but threatened to start again. We were seated beside a driveway, and we could see through an archway some thirty yards away into the museum courtyard. Douglas turned to me and asked, "Why is it raining in there and not out here?" I turned to explain that was probably not the case when I saw he was right. About a half minute later it began pouring on us.

It is still raining nearly every day, but usually not all day. We are learning to take rain gear with us no matter what the day looks like in the morning. We'll learn to live in England yet! We've got over three weeks to work at it. Scrabble tonight and early to bed.

TUESDAY, AUGUST 8

D.& D. both up about 8:30; I an hour later. By 11:00 we had had our breakfast and baths and were ready once again to take on the British Museum of Science. We spend another day just doing that. I finally felt about two o'clock that I just didn't care to know anymore. I had had enough physics, mathematics, glassmakiing, moon landings, x-ray technology, topology. Actually I was tired because I again did not sleep so well. That is unusual because I rarely have difficulty sleeping. My bed is too narrow and I seem to spend the night trying to get comfortable and to stay covered up. Every time I turn over I have to adjust the bedclothes, and in addition the bed is too soft for me. So I

36

sat down at every opportunity and was more than ready to come home when we left after five. Out to dinner; home to Scrabble.

Yesterday when we were walking through a tunnel leading from the museums to South Kensington Station, David saw an old man playing a harmonica asking passersby for whatever coins they might give him. David asked for money and I gave him and Douglas a penny each to put in the old man's hat. He seemed SO appreciative. God bless you," he said grabbing their hands and kissing them. "God bless you, little darlings." I thought he was going to cry. And so to bed.

WEDNESDAY, AUGUST 9TH

Rain again--of course. Mr. Clarke gave us a television set today . There go all the imaginative games, all the interaction, scrabble, perhaps even talking to each other at all. Douglas said he didn't feel well enough to go out today--but I wasn't having any of that. Mr. Clark said we could get an inside antenna and get all four channels. I decided not to get the antenna. Perhaps the two available channels will be so bad that we won't be tempted to watch television all the time. The good thing is that BBC does have some good programs. I saw an interesting program on Mexican Indians today and this evening another on child psychology.

We got out again to the British Museum of Science and finally finished it--or at least called a halt to working at finishing it. Some things you just don't finish--like strawberry pie, for example. I sat the day out in the children's section (where we were) and I watched lots of British women. They seemed so plain to me. So stolid. Pale and colorless. What indeed am I seeing? Can I generalize about the women I am seeing here at the British Museum of Science? I don't even think I know what I am seeing, who I am seeing, the extent to which I can or can't generalize about what and who I am seeing.

I do have some vague notion that the average worker makes more in the United States than in Britain. Is that true, and if it is true, what does it mean? What can I see with my eyes that will show that? In THE LONDON DAILY ADVERTISER I frequently see that a man might advertise for a wife and his main claim might be that he has a car or even a motorcycle. I don't think a man could hope to attract a wife with a car. A house, maybe, but not a car and certainly not a motorcycle. I think it might be easier to get a car in the U.S. I think that in general people have more in the U.S. than perhaps anywhere else in the world.

I met a very interesting and amusing woman here in the children's section of the museum. She was stylishly dressed, quite vivacious and humorous. About 45 years of age--I'd say. (right up there next to sixty as a great age for women). Quite attractive. She gave me her phone number and told me I should call her but I knew I wouldn't.. She was very funny and she had the boys laughing with her impersonations of a sad little girl who had been separated from her father at the museum. She did a little skit about the child's being lost but ultimately, by being very clever, using some things she had learned at the museum about directions, finding her 'Da.'

On the whole, British women begin to look more attractive to me the longer I am here. I see many gorgeous Asian, African, and Caribbean women too. I'm sure I'll have much more to say about this subject the longer I am here.

It seems quite customary to start up a conversation with anyone you sit next to in a museum or gallery. (Or at least anyone who sits or stands next to me seems to feel free to strike up a conversation.)

Douglas and David again gave money to the old man who plays the harmonica in the tunnel between the museum and Kensington

Station. His response is becoming downright embarrassing. The hand kissing, hugging, "God blesses," etc.

We are doing quite well with our budget. I have relaxed about money. I hope to find money from JoAnne tomorrow at American Express. In any case I've paid the rent for the next week and have enough for food and housing for a week beyond.

Tomorrow to Greenwich or the Tower.

THURSDAY, AUGUST 10

Finally got the gang out after lunch--about 1:30. We went to Picadilly Circus to American Express on Haymarket St. to pick up our money which I hope JoAnne has sent from my August 4th pay check. The money was not there nor was there any message of explanation. I will return the middle of next week and maybe that will be time enough for the money to have arrived. She is terribly busy and does have to travel all the way to downtown Princeton to get it off. Fortunately I do not need it immediately.

After we had gone to American Express, we went to the Victoria and Albert Museum. What an interesting potpourri of things there. Clothing of the nineteenth and early twentieth centuries. A wild costume, a recent acquisition, worn by Elton John in some recent concert. Paintings--some by well-known painters of the Renaissance and later. Statuary, religious articles--mitres, chalices, crosses made of precious metals--lots of pieces from China--nineteenth-century and earlier. I didn't get to see a great number of exhibitions because Douglas didn't want to go in the first place and from the moment we got there he began lobbying to go home. We compromised and he stayed a while anyway. He explained, "I'm just not interested in those things." Then we went home. He was sweet all evening. He even gave me an unsolicited hug.

We saw a very funny movie on T.V., "The House on Nightmare Park." David came up with a plan that would have us watching a maximum of one hour and forty-five minutes of television daily. I don't remember if it worked or not.]

FRIDAY, AUGUST 11

I can't believe that the weekend is here again. It seems only a day or so ago that it was Saturday. I am struck generally by my changed sense of time. The 25th of July--the day we arrived--seemed the longest day ever. The days in July all seemed long in comparison with recent days. I remember thinking earlier that July would never end. Well, not only did it end, but we are now nearly two weeks into August. Incredible!

I just finished another dime novel. I've been reading mysteries and detective stories that I got for 20 to 40 cents at the book store on the corner. I find them entertaining and relaxing.

I seem to be meditating less as I become more comfortable in this environment. At the moment I have nearly convinced myself that we are not going to run out of money and find ourselves on the street without resources, and that we will leave England in as orderly and planned a way as we arrived. The airline will not let us down, neither David nor Douglas will get lost; our passports and airline tickets will not be stolen or even misplaced. But how do you keep these things from happening if you don't think about them daily at least a million times? I suppose this is the first time I have ever been so much on my own without family or friend or some institution or another within helping distance. The realization has been rather surprising and frightening. I think I might be putting some finishing touches on the last stages of growing up. I think I am getting something I sorely need. Am I undergoing some final stage of maturation at my advanced age? If so, better now than never.

We went to Greenwich today by excursion boat on the Thames. We saw many historical sites that we would not otherwise have seen. The most impressive site, however, was not pointed out by the guide. That was the mile after mile of decayed wharves and abandoned, dilapidated warehouses--history in themselves of the turn in British fortunes in the twentieth century. The Thames teemed with freighters from all over the world not so long ago. But now all that is gone (well, not ALL of it), and only a few freighters are on the river at all. There was no vessel sailing in or out of port.

It is ironic that the people of the Commonwealth nations have now come to England to claim their birthright. English school masters in India, Africa, and Asia taught their charges that England was the greatest nation on earth and that their King or Queen lived "all across the big water." Now they have come themselves to experience the seat of Empire and Majesty.

How evident it is that the world has changed so very dramatically in the past fifteen years. It used to be that the American tourists drove the big cars, stayed at the big hotels, and ate at the same costly restaurants. Some Americans of course still do. But those fruits are shared by many, by the Italians, Germans, French, Japanese and middle easterners. The two Rolls Royces I saw today were driven by Japanese. If the Japanese were chauffeurs, were they drivers for other Japanese?

The trip to Greenwich was pleasant. We did not have enough time there though. We should have left by mid-morning. As it was, we scurried through the Cutty Sark and through the Maritime Museum. We needed at least two additional hours in order to have made the most of the visit. I'll need to pay more attention to planning. Good weather today. No rain! And so to bed.

Douglas today while doing dishes: "I hope I get out of this without dishpan hands."

SATURDAY, AUGUST 12

Not much doing today. Went out for a walk but came back when it started raining. Read junk fiction. Worried about money coming. Pizza at "Pizzaland." The waitress thought it hilariously funny when I sent my glass of beer back with the comment that it had lipstick on it and I wasn't wearing any. I suppose that the fact is not that I run out of things to write about, but that I don't always feel like writing. I wonder if the new Pope will be a woman, and it so, how will she be addressed?

SUNDAY, AUGUST 13

Not much doing today either. Generally we do not do much on weekends. Today I read another junk book--an exciting spy story. We went for a walk around the neighborhood looking for new places to eat and in general to see more of what surrounds us. Found out where the Sunday flea market is and I will go there next Sunday morning. Played Scrabble in the late afternoon before dinner.

WEEK FOUR

MONDAY, AUGUST 14

We have fallen into such a rigid, iron-clad routine that I must do something to change it. I'll have to call upon my imagination to vary our diet for example. I did add boiled eggs to breakfast and soup for lunch. Still our main sustenance is bread and cheese. We are drinking less tea. I find the least bit of caffeinated tea gives me the shakes since I was having a cup or two of strong tea our first few mornings here. That undoubtedly sent me up pretty high.

Still the best place to eat seems the New Hot Pot. We get a full, satisfying meal for less than 3 pounds for the three of us. In order that the fare to get there not be wasted I planned that we would go to Trafalgar Square--a fairly close distance from Picadilly Circus. We walked there, saw the statue of Lord Nelson high atop its tall pedestal. The National Gallery is on the square. We went through it--hurriedly, but not so hurriedly that I was unable to appreciate the marvelous collection there. There are many paintings from the renaissance through to the nineteenth century: Rembrandt, daVinci, Reubens, Van Dyck, Van Gogh, Titian and countless others. It is a marvelous collection--nearly as many guards as viewers.

The kids were very patient. Douglas did not once complain. In fact he said sympathetically to me: "Perhaps we can come back and see more another day." We walked around the square, back to Picadilly Circus and took the train back home.

I'll call JoAnne tonight and find out why we don't have our money. If I could just manage not to worry about everything so damned much!!

TUESDAY, AUGUST 15

Last night (Monday) we decided to call JoAnne. We stayed up 'til midnight, six o'clock PM in New Jersey--and called. We got no answer and went to bed. We decided to call about 1:30PM on Tuesday--7:30AM in New Jersey. But when we called the operator told us that a labor dispute was on and it was unlikely we would get through for several days. THAT threw me into a really deep funk. I had no idea whether ANY of my letters had got through. Watched TV. Went to bed.

Not. much doing today. But of course I am worried about money again. We have enough to last until one week from Wednesday at our careful, frugal rate. I was in a deep funk most of the day. The boys seemed to sense this and seemed most solicitous toward me. I meditated for some time and by early afternoon felt considerably more self-assured. We went out to buy books, returned and spent the afternoon reading.

WEDNESDAY, AUGUST 16

Woke up at 5:30 AM and decided to try JoAnne again. I had seen on T.V. that many overseas lines were out entirely--there is no telephone contact between Britain and several countries, and lines between Britain and the U.S. are overloaded. When I called on Monday night I didn't know about the problem but I did get the number even though there was no answer. I figured there was a good chance that at 6 AM here and 12 midnight there was a good chance of getting through.

I indeed did. JoAnne told me she had sent the money on Monday and I should receive a telegraph to that effect. She urged me to go to France. Assuming I will get the money tomorrow--or Friday. the trip now seems to appear viable. I will take David and Doug for 5-7 days.

If I'm paying about $20-25 per day here and that's absolute maximum--can't pay more--I can make out. Breakfast and lunch at home or one meal or picnic; one restaurant meal. . I've looked everywhere and I can't find a cheaper, trustworthy place to eat. But the money is coming. If not, I'll try to worry with greater urgency and efficiency.

We went to a movie today up North at Kilburn. That is a much poorer area (or so it seems to me) than Earls' Court where we live. Restaurant prices are, however, no less. We saw <u>Candleshoe</u> and <u>Alice in Wonderland.</u> I enjoyed them both; I think we all did. Back about 6PM and so right to supper.

When we returned, Douglas was unhappy because he had nothing to read while David and I did. So I wrote him a story, "The Mystery of the Earl's Court Station Monster." He asked me to write another one--twenty pages instead of six. I guess I will. T.V. on and soon to bed. Oh, one more thing. I changed money today. My last $200 and the dollar is doing so poorly that I got over three pounds less in exchange than I got a week before for the same dollar amount. Grr!!

THURSDAY, AUGUST 17

Today was a boring day. I didn't feel like doing anything. (This must be the way Douglas feels sometimes.) I stayed in and except for my usual morning shopping excursion, did nothing but read all day.

We are around so many non-English speaking people that I frequently have to remind myself what country I am in. I find myself often speaking slowly and distinctly to everybody.

The novel I read today, William Price Fox's RUBY RED, was not a bad book even though it cost only 20p. I recall that I knew Fox when I was at the University of Iowa briefly in 1970-71.

Got a telegram from JoAnne yesterday saying that the money will be at Chase Manhattan bank at Woolgate House, Coleman Street. I decided to give it an extra day and go there tomorrow.

Douglas said he did not like Alice in Wonderland and that he did not want to see it. (He did like Candleshoe.) Furthermore there isn't much in London that he does like. I think he misses his Mum and the familiar surroundings of home and town. He doesn't say so-- doesn't even say he wants to go home anymore, and when I said we would probably leave on September 4, he said he hoped we would leave later in the week--on the 8th or 9th.

His little feelings about where he wants to be are probably all ajumble--just as my little feelings are. I really felt on last Sunday morning when I thought of all my friends in Princeton--everybody out playing tennis - that I really wanted to be at home. But I quickly changed my mind.

I do hope I keep in shape with all the walking we do. I am also watching my diet--not eating a great deal and balancing the proteins and carbohydrates. I think Douglas is losing weight. He is of his own accord eating considerably less. David seems to stay about the same though he eats a good amount. They are eating far fewer sweets and there are practically no snacks except for the greengage plums I have been buying of late. We are all on better diets. Not eating at all between meals. Since I've been here I've had two glasses of wine and four pints of beer. But that has been because I'm doing my part in keeping costs down. We are trying hard to keep our evening meal to 3 pounds or less. Since the boys are doing a lot, I can hardly do less.

We are getting out early tomorrow and going to Westminster Abbey and later we'll go to Chase Manhattan. If there is time, I'll check out possibilities for France at a travel agency. I hope the boys can take advantage of student rates. I wonder if you have to be college-age to do that?

FRIDAY, AUGUST 18

How time is flying. The days tick by like seconds on a clock. We went out early today--early for us--at 11o'clock. Before we could get on the train at Earl's Court Station the overripe pears we were carrying along for lunch squished and we had a grand mess on our hands. All over cameras, raincoats, umbrella! We went along to Parliament Square where I bought tissues to clean up.

Then on to St. Margaret's church where loads of people were doing brass rubbings. Not the kind of thing I felt inclined to do. We went on to Westminster Abbey and spent a good deal of time there among the dead and among the living - crowding through to see the tombs of the dead. It was interesting to see the tombs of the famous, but most of the dead there are people I've never heard of and could care less whether they are buried there or in a pauper's graveyard. I suspect you must have money to be buried in the Abbey. But it did seem that most of those buried there are people I've never heard of and I could care less about their being buried there than they might care about my being buried there. Their bodies are probably useful however, as monuments to history, British History and world history as conceived through British and western eyes.

As we passed into the Abbey some character in a red frock turned on my little boys and exclaimed in a high screeching voice: "Take your hats off!" His eyes gleamed with his pleasure in exerting authority that day. On his way home, I fantasize happily, he trips and scrapes his shin on a curb. It's very painful. That'll show 'im. Never underestimate the power of my imagination. And my pen!

There is a curious split here in Britain--perhaps not so curious as more obvious here--between an idea of the country and what it really is or has been. There is the lofty ideal of King or Queen, of nobility, of a glorious past whose influence stretches into the present--an ideal far more firmly implanted in the souls of the people than the American ideal, for example, is planted in the souls of the American people. But somehow or another I find it at best difficult to separate the ideas of Buckingham Palace the implications of the new pictures of Princess Anne and her baby, the Queen and the old watery eyed man I saw at the British Museum of Natural History picking through a trash can, or the little old toothless and nearly blind, obviously very poor man who delivered my telegram yesterday.

On the surface there is an idealized sense of reality which masks poverty, cruelty, ugliness, meanness, avariciousness--all these quite human characteristics which have always been with us. Clearly that schizophrenic view is apparent in British history. "The sun never sets on the British Empire, "God save the Queen (and that toothless, old telegraph messenger too, especially him; he needs help more than she.")

We crossed the river and ate lunch near the London County Hall. We left there for the tube station. I called Chase Manhattan only to learn they closed at three. We'll have to go on Monday to get our money. I'm sure it's there, but I'm continuing on our program of economy and frugality. I'll believe we have the money when it is in my hands.

We had a sock fight before bed, an ancient sport that allows great alleviation of tensions of all kinds before bed. You roll up four long socks and pelt each other with them mercilessly--the boys against their father. Great fun. Greatly relieves tensions. Somehow one naturally knows when the fight begins and when it ends. There's never a question of start or finish--self-regulating, it comes and goes of its own volition.

SATURDAY, AUGUST 19

Nothing much doing today. Quiet, mostly reading. Bought books at corner. Ate later tonight. Finished <u>The Cross of Frankenstein</u>. The book was as much my cross as his.

SUNDAY, AUGUST 20

Went to Flea Market. Mostly cheap junk. Shiny aluminum tea sets. Bright gold-colored jewelry with fake stones, plastic purses and luggage--real cheap junk. Found nothing worth buying. Tried to call the Johnson's friends, the McMillans. Information won't answer. Maybe it's closed on Sunday. Messed around for the rest of the day. Dinner--sock fight, scrabble, reading, bed.

WEEK FIVE

MONDAY, AUGUST 21

Busy day today. It took hours to get dressed, have breakfast, and get out. I was still anxious about getting the money even though JoAnne had told me it was sent and I even had the telegram to that effect. But knowing as I do the vicissitudes of life. . . perhaps I should say "fearing as I do. . . ." We finally got to Bank Station, found Coleman street and--after waiting and signing 95 forms--I got the money. Much relieved!

Now I could spend the day worrying whether someone was going to pick one pocket (passport); another (wallet); a third (traveller's checks). I might even have relaxed if I had noted that I'd already been robbed at Chase Manhattan: $3 for American Express Travelers' checks after they had converted the money to pounds and charged me a conversion fee.

We then went on to Tower Hill to the Tower of London. As we went in I once again had a tiff with a guard. David had our Ho-Ho-Ho bag. I was standing with David as the guard said, "Move along." I lingered waiting for David. At the end of the table I heard the guard say to another, "I told him [me] to move along three times." I said loudly - perhaps louder than I needed to, "I'm waiting for my son!" "You don't have a bag, do you? he asked. "I don't, but my son does. And that's why I'm waiting." "Move along!" he shouted. By that · time David was through the line. I was pretty angry. When the guard goes home, I imagined strenuously, he'll fall and scrape his forehead on a bench. I'll just have him hurt himself a bit.... terribly painful! Ah fantasy! It is thus that I mete out justice on behalf of my boys.

We saw the "Bloody Tower" where Edward II had the two children murdered. And we saw the crown jewels. Wow!! Really something. Such diamonds, rubies, emeralds. More jewels than I'd ever seen. We went through the white tower where David finally got to see his armor. Lots of guns from the 14th century on. The British are a militaristic people. Guns, weapons, armaments everywhere. I guess no more so than others. We had lunch outside on a bench.

On our way back to the tube station we saw a street show. It was pretty hokey. An escape show performed by a man who had the biggest belly in captivity. After I saw him I decided not to eat for two days.

Back home. Sock fight. David jumped on the bed and a leg collapsed. I'll have to tell the caretaker before we leave.

TUESDAY, AUGUST 22

Called Air India this morning and and found out we are leaving on Monday, Sept. 4th at 1 PM. I tried to find out whether New York Airways was going to transport.us by helicopter between J.F.K and Newark Int. as they had on our way here. I couldn't find out, so I'll just act as though we're returning the same way we came and see what happens.

My plan for the morning was to go to Victoria Coach Station and buy bus tickets to Paris. I called yesterday and found out that is the cheapest way to go. $124 for the three of us. For some unknown reason I happened to decide to look at my passport. Horrors!!! Staring me in the face where my face should have been was the face of one Catherine Drozdowski!! They had given me the wrong passport at the bank yesterday! The fantasies began. I could see old Caty tooling off to Northern Ireland for the summer--or being in London for the summer but not looking at her passport for the next month. I rushed the kids back in record time (an hour and a half) and we went back to Bank Station and Chase Manhattan. We walked in and the receptionist knew immediately who I was and the teller who had made the error was overjoyed. Apparently Caty had planned to leave for the states tomorrow. I actually knew I would be able to get another passport, but who wants to go through all that?

"I'm so sorry," the teller said.

"It's nothing," said I, lying through my teeth. "Passports do tend to get lost sometimes."

We then went to Victoria Coach Station and I made reservations for Paris. We leave next Sunday, 10:15 PM . While I waited two men came in and insinuated themselves in front of me in the queue. When we got near the ticket agent, I simply stepped in front of them saying, "I believe I was here before you gentlemen."

"He was indeed," one of them said.

Back home. Bought a luggage cart so we can move about more easily. I'll call JoAnne in the morning to ask what's going on with the next gold shipment. She said she would send it last Friday, but no sign of it so far. I'll have enough to keep us here, but I'm going to need more since we're going to France afterall. I've got $300. but we've still got 12 days to go and that's not enough. I reserved a room at the YWCA for two days prior to departure from London. Wrote cards to more friends. David and Douglas did too.

We are all losing weight. My shirt today felt like a sack. We are eating less but getting our vitamins and properly balanced meals. We are eating well but simply. I Hope we can keep it up when we return home. No complaints about food either.

Started Margaret Drabble's <u>The Needle's Eye.</u> Thought I'd read a <u>good</u> book for a change. The mystery I finished last night, <u>The Tower Room</u>, was not a bad book, but the ending was simply miserable. I checked the prices of about five of M. Drabble's books. I'm right! They're sold by the pound.

I'm getting excited about going to Paris. We don't have accommodations there, but we'll get there on a Monday morning and have lots of time to find a place. A Monday morning should be a good time to arrive. Lots of leads from <u>FROMMER'S</u>.

WEDNESDAY, AUGUST 23

The other day Douglas declared that he is not a sight-seer, that he does not particularly enjoy going to see things. I am about to agree with him. I think I am getting my fill of sight-seeing too. I suppose I will do more next week in Paris. It certainly isn't possible to go to Paris and NOT sightsee. After seeing so much one probably needs time to assimilate it all, if not time simply to rest adequately one's mind and body. I will make sure that we visit the major Paris sights, but I don't plan to be tearing around the city trying to take in everything.

We called JoAnne at six-o'clock this morning. She is going to send money to Paris. I had hoped she would have sent it here to London, but I'm sure it will work just as well to send it to Paris. I will be going to Paris with $150 and that won't last too long. Then I want to have money to buy presents in France and in England when we return. I have bought practically nothing so far other than necessities. I'm not secure enough to feel that I'm going to have what I need when I need it.

JoAnne said that my old friend Bill Moynihan will be in Paris. I wish I knew how to get in touch with him. I've hardly talked with another adult in a good while. (As I'm revising this it occurs to me that I don't know whether Bill Moynihan was indeed in Paris at this time. I suspect I'll never know.)

After we'd got up early to call JoAnne we didn't go back to sleep. We stayed in napping and reading until dinner time. D & D have gone back to inventing games which they did for some time today. They watch TV a reasonable amount of time each day but by no means all day. I am pleased about that.

The M. Drabble book, <u>The Needle's Eye</u>, is quite fascinating. The extraordinarily developed detail of the lives of her characters is painful to witness because I can't but feel that she suffers along with her characters. She knows too much. I only know one life as well as she knows the full and complete lives of her two central characters--and that is my own, and I'm not so sure that I know that life as well as she knows the full and complete lives of the two central characters.. I don't even want to know other lives as well as I know my own, I couldn't bear it.

Douglas: (In a little whisper as I lay on my bed one afternoon): "Dad, are you asleep?"
David: "Of course he's not asleep. He's meditating. Dad never sleeps on his back!"

Hope I can find an inexpensive good play to take the boys to.

THURSDAY, AUGUST 24

Once again I am afraid to spend any money. The prospect of going to France with only the $150 I currently have in traveller's checks leaves me uncomfortable. I can't believe that the $490 I got last Monday is nearly gone. Fare to France, daily living expense, prepaid reservation for when we return has left me the aforementioned $150, plus 35 pounds. Three more days to go, and I'll want to have some money for the trip. We'll take food along but I'm sure I'll have to buy <u>something</u>.

In the morning we wrote postcards and read. Douglas had bought a book called <u>How to Catch More Eels</u> and he's interested in becoming a catcher of large eels. In reading about them we've discovered that eel's blood is toxic and dangerous if it enters an open wound or gets into the eyes. Cooking (heat) destroys the toxicity. I"d better start looking for eel recipes. Imagine: sauteed eel with mushrooms; eel flambe, spaghetti with eel sauce--there must be many, many eel recipes we don't know about yet. Haven't even imagined.

We bought a deck of cards and I taught D. & D. to play poker. We played for the whole afternoon, and they continued to play into the evening. Douglas has a knack for the game and he asked if he could invite his friends over to play when we return. I told him that he could not play for money and that some parents might not want their children to learn the game at all. He later asked if he could invite his friend Bruce over and teach him the game without telling him what it was. I suggested that this might not be a good thing to do and tried to think up a few reasons.

I think I'm getting the point of <u>The Needle's Eye</u>. Of course things may change--I'm only half way through the book. What's happening is that the main characters are being presented in such a way as to preclude negative judgment on the reader's part of them and of the affair they are headed toward. No one is at fault in these things-- they simply happen as the result of circumstances and early environment. "No fault." It is not that the characters do not have flaws-- they do. But their flaws are integral parts of their characters and are influential in the molding of their circumstances. The interesting aspect of the novel is the author's expression of judgment in a context which on the surface seems free of the expression of moral, philosophical and social norms. We'll see whether my thoughts hold up through the second half of the novel.

Must find something to do tomorrow that won't cost much. Maybe an outdoor concert if I can find one.

FRIDAY, AUGUST 25

No outdoor concert--no nothing. I can't seem to get out--at least any further than the market or the laundromat. I am AGAIN nearly paralyzed with fear at the thought of finding myself totally without money either in France or here when we return in a week. I suppose I simply do not have the confidence necessary to feel assured that my money will be forthcoming. The prospect of having as little money in Paris as I will have if J. fails to send the money is not very pleasant. So I suppose I sit inside not because I'm paralyzed (which might be cause for REAL alarm), but to avoid spending any more than I absolutely must for health's and cleanliness's sake.

If I had any sense I would know that I needn't worry about JoAnne holding up her end as long as these two boys (her children) are with me. She will move heaven and earth for the sake of their well-being.

I read and played cards with the children all day. They are enjoying playing cards and seem not to mind not going sight-seeing. They don't seem particularly restless or irritable but quite satisfied with each other's company and the amusements we devise together. I could not ask that they be better behaved. It seems as though they somehow know that I need them to be well behaved at this time. Because I have an underlying feeling of guilt because I am not taking the children about right now, I suppose that another way of looking at it is to realize that we are spending more consistent time together than we have spent for the past two and one-half years. I felt that I certainly knew them before this trip, having seen them as frequently a I have, but I know more about them than I did, and I am sure that works both ways. Certainly one function of this trip has been for them to spend an unbroken length of time with their father and conversely. From this perspective I do not mind at all that our attention is focused on each other instead of upon some monument, gravesite, or historic plain. We probably have, so far, achieved a not-unreasonable balance.

A reasonable perspective on our trip to Paris: Our fare is paid both ways. I will get the least expensive, decent hotel I can; I will establish a budget that will allow us to survive on what I have now. Our breakfasts are included at the YWCA when we return. I will save enough for food of some kind on Saturday and Sunday, September 2 and 3. We will simply do what we can and must.

SATURDAY, AUGUST 26

Stayed in all day except for morning shopping and dinner. Taught the boys to play whist. Read. They watched the Olympics on TV and other sports programs. Called JoAnne about 7PM--no answer. I have no profound observations to make today. It is now 8:45PM. I will call again later.

Douglas complains of a painful backache.

Called JoAnne at midnight and then tried again at 6:45AM. Telephone turned off! What phone? Not sure as of this writing. Will try again this evening.

Still Saturday. Meanwhile I watched a lousy movie. Richard Burton--called The Villain. It was the worst movie I have ever seen. I couldn't tell who was worse, the character of the villain in the fictional piece or the character of Burton himself for accepting such an awful characterless (if there can be such a thing) role. Unbelievable plot. Bad photography. Off to Paris tomorrow.

Donald B. Gibson

WEEK SIX

MONDAY, AUGUST 28

Telescoping these two days because we didn't sleep in a bed Sunday night and the one day simply flowed into the next with no break. (Later as I go over this journal ...I don't understand this. "Didn't sleep in a bed?" What did we do?)

We prepared to leave today. Amazing how much effort and energy it takes to pack up--especially given the fact we never totally unpacked. We used two drawers in the chest, hung up some things, and left others in the bags. In any event I spent a good part of the day packing and cleaning. It probably seemed to be so much because I did it in spurts while doing other things which were part of our daily routine.

One thing that we spent a lot of time doing is playing poker. The boys have really taken to it! I hope I have't created a monster. Or two! But it will probably be like many other enthusiasms since we've been abroad, enthusiasms which are at first of utter intensity but which diminish, waning with the passage of time. Perhaps I shouldn't worry about this one. (I speak many years hence and I tell you gambling was never a problem with them. They both turned out OK.)

D and D. cleaned up our Earl's Court flat for the last time. They have been very good about fulfilling their responsibility to the job they assigned themselves of keeping the apartment up on a daily basis.

Though they have occasionally needed prodding, they have performed their tasks with proficiency on nearly a daily basis. I was surprised at how they took this place and their circumstances as responsibilities. They never complained about having to go across the hall to the loo. They did not like having to go all the way to the first floor for a shower (after the one on the floor below slipped into disrepair). They did not particularly like that the first floor shower was largely public; that is, it is a large room with two curtained showers and a toilet at one end (enclosed).

All facilities are used by others in the building--men, women, and children-- at various times. They are not used to such proximity among strangers in bathing and they did not like it. Also the place, though not filthy, is not the cleanest imaginable. There are no bugs or rodents; the trash is emptied daily, and the halls are vacuumed. But it is a bit dark and dingy and sorely needs a coat of paint. There is not sufficient lighting at night, but it is light enough during the day. Well, goodbye to all that.

I paid for the room for an extra day because our bus was not scheduled to leave until 10:15PM, Sunday night and I did not want to hang out on the street somewhere simply passing the time away. We had dinner and left for the station at about 8PM. Our new luggage carrier helped considerably but the luggage was still a struggle. It had two bags on it and though the carrier helped considerably on level ground, it had to be carried up and down stairs. (Years later I think of the suitcases on wheels that have become common since those days!)

We made it to Victoria Station. Fortunately the tube was uncrowded at that hour. Then we traveled the several blocks to Victoria Coach Station. We boarded our bus to Paris about 9:45. I heard a young girl (14 or 15) bidding goodbye to her friends in some odd but familiar language. It took me a moment to recognize it as

Polish. (I lived in Poland for two years in the early 60's--but that's another story.)

The trip from London to Dover was quite fast--a couple of hours? In towns along the way I saw large numbers of Indians and other dark-skinned people, Africans I would say, on the street, occasionally in pubs, but not very often (for what that's worth given the little I could see from my bus window-- vantage point).

During my stay in London I encountered only a few instances of overt racism. In a restaurant I heard a raucous and generally obnoxious Englishman address an Indian who was waiting for a table as "Steamboat." Graffiti on a wall had been revised . "niggers out" had been edited rather humorously to read "sniggers snout," far more effective than crossing it out. Once on our way to Victoria Coach Station one of a group of teenagers rushing by said to David, "Where you going, Boss?" (Racist?) Another in the group said to the speaker, "What are you talking about?"--a kind of apology--as I read it-- to his foreign visitors. I also saw written on a tube station wall: "Punch a Paki." Whether there was more there or not (I'm sure there was) that's all I saw.

We boarded the ferry at Dover and I was sorry that the cliffs were not visible. Perhaps they will be on the way back. I spoke in Polish to the girl who had boarded our bus in London. She was of course shocked that I spoke her language. We chatted, she largely speaking of how awful Poland was and I defending it. I had the strong feeling that she was largely attacking it out of shame about the country's material deficiencies. I was able to deflect her perspective in such a way as to have a far more pleasant conversation talking about what I admired about Poles and about Poland. This largely had to do with the great joy I had in meeting so many Polish people, about the many, many Polish friends I had and how many of them had visited me in the United States. She found it humorous that I had to hire a Polish tutor because everyone wanted to speak with me in English and I had to pay several tutors to converse with me in Polish.

The trip from Calais to Paris in the early A.M. was lovely. D.& D. and I had been on the verge of seasickness and perhaps part of my positive response is attributable to having the crossing done with. In any case I saw the sun rise and the lovely little distant villages and the dark greens and yellows of the country side were quite beautiful. I dozed part of the time as did D & D. Our bus was scheduled to arrive in Paris at Gare St. Lazare at 9:45AM.

At 9:30, however, a young English woman had gone to the front of the bus to ask the driver if he was sure of the route. Before we boarded the bus in London I had heard the driver say to the clerk checking in passengers that this was his first trip to Paris. I said to David at the time, "I wonder if we're going to get lost?" By 10:45 we had found the general area of Gare St.Lazare where we should be, but the driver couldn't find where to discharge passengers. I was anxious to know where the point of disembarkation was so I'd know where to board the bus for the trip back. We kept going around in circles and finally by 11:30 the driver had, by some means or another, found the right place.

We gathered the luggage, I exchanged money ($130 in French francs for my $150 in travelers'checks!). Then we tackled the subway. I refused to give in to my urge to say "The hell with it" and take a taxi. But what an ordeal! It wouldn't have been so bad if we hadn't had the luggage. As it was we had a sore trial getting through the underground maze, largely because there were so many stairs. Also we were frantic about getting on and off the coaches before the doors closed on us. I was carrying the big suitcase and the Ho-Ho-Ho bag with our cameras, food, and other things. David and Doug were alternately managing the luggage carrier but I had to help them on and off the coaches by lifting the carrier.

After we got to our destination, Maubert -Mutualite, we then had to find a hotel. After our lack of success at the first three places, we then went to Rue Des Ecoles and I sat the children down on the campus of one of the colleges while I went off into the next block to search for a place. Every place was too expensive--a good 15 to 20% higher than Frommer had promised me. Finally at the Hotel des Grand Nations I settled for a place for 115f after the manager was convinced I was not going to pay any more. That was about what everybody on the street is asking. Of course the rooms available are all with toilet and shower--since those are the hardest to rent out.

It was a great relief to be settled, but an even greater relief when I called JoAnne and found that she had wired money last Thursday to American Express, Paris. If I'd only kept in mind that I had hostages, I would have known that JoAnne would move heaven and earth to insure that her two sons were denied nothing they needed.

We were all exhausted and took a rest until 8:00PM. We then went out to the restaurant below. I had veal, salad, and wine. The boys had Pizza, Calzone, and dessert. 84 F. $16.50. Tomorrow we find cheap places to eat. Small consolation: the daily cost we pay here includes breakfast!

INTERESTING OBSERVATION: As we were wending our way to our hotel (the Hotel de Grand Nations) a number of people, (seven) at different points, seeing us struggling with our luggage, gave us, unbidden, a hand. Four helped with the carrying of the luggage; three with directions (even though we hadn't asked). One of the seven was French. Three were French-speaking Africans, two were Asians and two were young British women, tourists. How very thankful I was and still am. Even after all these years. What a day this was. I took a long hot shower and we all went immediately to bed.

TUESDAY, AUGUST 29

Breakfast is served in our room at the hotel. At the rate we are paying they should chew it and digest it for us as well. But it was a nice breakfast! Croissants, jam, butter and hot chocolate. We headed for American Express about eleven. We felt our way through the streets toward Rue Scribe and finally, painstakingly, made it there. The Paris underground system leaves me a bit confused. David seems to have little trouble with it. He very quickly learns how to get around the city on it via underground. He seems to have an extraordinary sense of direction. We never feel lost or even that we are likely to get lost.

We retrieved our money at American Express, and afterward sat for an enjoyable hour on the Place de l'Opera at an outside table of the New World restaurant. We then took the subway intending to go to the Eiffel Tower. We never made it. Instead we found ourselves at the Arc de Triumph. We took a long roundabout walk down the Champs Elysees and decided by mid-afternoon to return to our hotel, taking the long walk back. We had a lunch of bread and cheese--and I took a brief nap.

We had decided to go that evening to see the Marx Brothers movie, Duck Soup, but by the time we were ready to eat, about 5:45, it was clear we couldn't eat and get to the movie by seven. So we decided to walk about until 7:00, see the movie and then have dinner. (Let me skip ahead until after the movie.) We went to a Vietnamese restaurant. The food was good but since I didn't know the restaurant well, I wasn't sure we were having the best that the restaurant had to offer. I hope we'll get back there again. The place was very crowded and the meal took about two hours. The waiters were Vietnamese. I could not understand a word of their French and they understood less of mine.

I had seen <u>Duck Soup</u> before, but I don't think I had ever seen it in a movie theater. It was totally a scream!! I was nearly rolling in the aisles--we all were. I hadn't laughed so long for a very, very long time. We were nearly hysterical. Quite a release to laugh so much.

After the movie we went home and played poker. They boys cleaned me out. Good thing we're not playing for real money. It is very exciting to be in France. Earlier I wrote:
France is a much more lively and inviting country than England. I like it better. Paris is indeed "la plus belle ville du mond." The women are georgeous. The only fat people are tourists. Ok, so maybe this isn't true and and if so I deny having said it. It only reflects the excitement of our first days.

WEDNESDAY, AUGUST 30

Today the boys did not want to go out sightseeing. I should by now recognize that they are establishing a pace. I should have expected that after the energy they expended getting here they would have needed recuperation time. The trip here from Gare St. La Zare was a very exhausting endeavor. They did not complain, but that doesn't mean they didn't feel something of the anxiety and pressure that I felt.

They seem here, as in London, to strive toward routine, to regularize existence, to establish similar patterns of behavior in any particular circumstance. Insight: That is the meaning of the games they create and play for hours on end. I have a certain image of what one does in visiting a foreign country. That image they do not have. They do not feel the need to go out and <u>do</u>. They react simply to <u>being</u> in the different environment, getting themselves together internally, slowly venturing out, returning home, assimilating with their games that allow them to integrate into the new environment. I do something like this too. There was a reason that today they stayed inside until nearly seven. I went out twice to walk and explore. In the afternoon I napped from 3:30 to 6:30. I did not feel like tackling the metro again today. I did not mind not doing much of a sight-seeing venture. The physiological facts find conjunction with the psychic reality.

They were, though, very happy to go to a movie again. We saw another Marx Bros. film at the cinema down the street. We saw Monkey Business--funny. but nowhere near as funny as Duck Soup.

After the movie we went to the same restaurant we went to last night. There was a wait so we went to another Vietnamese restaurant. We had the best meal we've had so far during our trip; for the first time we ate without paying so much attention to prices. We were not totally heedless of prices, but far less scrupulous. The meal lasted over two hours, but since we felt so comfortable, we enjoyed spending the time. The children want to go there again tomorrow night. We'll see.

Poker again until bed. They are becoming quite expert.

THURSDAY, AUGUST 31

Oh, what a day! Both boys are sick. Temperatures, runny noses, sore throats, coughs. Quelle dommage! Got post cards, but nobody feels like writing. Mailed mine off and bought cheese, bread, etc. for lunch. Boys felt better in the evening so we went to see A Night at the Opera. Very funny. Out to dinner at the same restaurant we went to last night. Douglas had banana flambe for dessert.

This morning when breakfast was brought up, David was showering so we sat his tray on a table. Douglas and I were eating when Douglas pointed toward David's tray and said, "What's that?" It was a roach! I killed it, but it destroyed all appetite for breakfast. None of us were unaffected by that.

Donald B. Gibson

FRIDAY AND SATURDAY, SEPTEMBER 1 AND 2

The troops feel better today. At breakfast nobody seems hungry. (I wonder why?) Nobody eats a single piece of bread and nobody says a word about why.

We went out early (11:00) to complete our sight-seeing of what we feel are the major Paris landmarks. Notre Dame is within walking distance, so we go there first, walk around, take a few pictures. Then on to the Louvre. We are doing a great deal of walking because I can't match the maps with our surroundings. That's fine with me though.

The Louvre is impossible. What can one do when there is so little time and so much more to see? I decide that we will see the Mona Lisa and tarry along the way coming and going to that. Catch as catch can. We see the Mona Lisa. I would never have gone to see it if I had been on my own. I would not have tried to do so much in so little time. I am glad, however, that I saw it and that David and Douglas saw it. I was not enraptured. Its notoriety had for me diminished the actual experience of it.

We left the Louvre. (Douglas made the pun: Louvre--loo). David with his increasingly unerring instinct for direction (knowing where he is and how to get where he wants to be) led us to the Eiffel Tower. We looked at that from a distance and then decided we first would go to the Aquarium, a short distance away. We went to the Marine Museum and what we thought was the Aquarium only to discover a high and distant view of the Eiffel Tower that we had not known or expected.

On this high hill, on an expanse of plaza, there were 40 or 50 black Algerians selling costume jewelry. Nearly all were selling the same fake ivory, fake silver, plastic busts and do-dads. I did not know what I was seeing. Were they indeed in competition with each other?

Or was this some kind of collective , communal activity? Do they go home each evening and divide up their profits?

We could not find the Aquarium but David and Douglas were determined. I was ready to go home because I was beginning to get antsy about packing for our journey to London, getting dinner, and then arriving at the station early enough to make sure we were at the right place to get on the bus to London.   Since they seemed determined, doggedly determined to find it, I suppressed my anxiety and sure enough they discovered it--not at the top of the hill, as we had supposed--but at the bottom. We saw the rather small collection of fish. The whole tour took no more than half an hour. They agreed that we should not take the time to walk all the way to the Eiffel Tower, but we might walk a bit closer.

We returned home (funny how a hotel room in a short time becomes "home") packed, had dinner, then headed off--with two hours leeway--to the Gare St. Lazare to find our bus/ferry to London. We were indeed in the right place.   The bus appeared at 9:50PM; we departed the station at 10:15 and were soon asleep.

We were scheduled to get into London, to Victoria Coach station, at 7:30AM. As it was we got in at 5:30AM. Instead of having half an hour to wait before we could go to our room at the YWCA, we had two and one-half hours. We sat in the station canteen. Around 6:30 or so I suggested we play cards--so we did that. Later Douglas began playing solitaire. At 7:55 I suggested we head out toward our hotel. We checked into the YWCA, locked our baggage away, then began the long wait for 12:30, the hour we would be admitted to our room.

In retrospect it doesn't seem as though we waited long at all. We went out and had breakfast, bought bread and cheese for lunch, then while I was out, I called The Irish Shop where I could find the sweater JoAnne asked me to get for her. I asked the hotel clerk where the shop was located. He said, "At Juke and _____." "Juke?" I asked. "Yes," he said. "Juke." How do you spell that," I asked. "J-u-k-e," he said. "Juke!" After I hung up I realized he was saying, "Duke," not "Juke."

Back at the YWCA we were admitted to our room, watched television and I took a nap in the early afternoon. Afterwards we talked with several people in the lounge. I was especially moved by a woman - Jackie who was on crutches after an incident of an unfortunate character occurring several days before. A gang of teenagers had begun to harass her as she approached. As she drew abreast one of them shoved against her for no reason at all, knocking her against a post and to the ground. They ran off laughing. Her eye was terribly swollen and blackened. She said that it was only in the past day or two that she had gained the confidence to walk any distance at all. Now she feels terrified to go out again. We were horrified.

For dinner we went to a little restaurant in a hotel up the street. I should have known better than to go into a place called "Eats." Here we finally found the meal that epitomized what was surely the worst eating experience in all of Britain. I had chicken and ham pie with peas, mashed potatoes and gravy. David had chicken in a basket with chips. Doug had a toasted ham and cheese sandwich. My dinner was awful! But eating mine was the more difficult because I first looked at David's. His chicken was dripping with grease. The leg had feathers on it, and if this wasn't enough, it was raw at the bone. David took one bite and said his stomach hurt. He said it tasted like fish. It had probably been fried in oil that fish had been fried in. Since my dinner had no discernible taste, I could not eat it without imagining it tasted like what I imagined David's tasted like. Hopefully we'll do better tomorrow night.

SUNDAY, SEPTEMBER 3

We got up this morning at 7:30--I should say we <u>woke</u> up in order to get our breakfast before 8:15AM. This was-a simpler meal here than at Arden House--but satisfactory. Tea, toast, cornflakes, a boiled egg, and marmalade.

After breakfast we went into the lounge. There is a group that regularly gathers there. Jackie, our new friend on crutches, was the center of it. Jackie is not able to move freely about, and spends a good deal of her time in the lounge. She has been quite friendly to us since we came. She is about 45 and she is, by profession a mid-wife. She is not highly educated but is very pleasant and she extends herself easily to others. She got along well with D. and D. They both liked her--responded positively to her.

We sat in the lounge, I thinking about whether we would indeed go to Hampton Court. Douglas did not want to go out at all. David did-- until I said we were taking the Green Line bus. "Oh, no," he said. I don't want to get on another bus."

So it was settled. We decided to spend a leisurely Sunday. I didn't mind that since we were still a bit tired from our Paris trip. Besides it was Sunday and everybody and his mother would be out on this day. . I napped and watched T.V. and Douglas did too. David sat up all day--no nap for him. In the evening we went out to dinner to a middle-Eastern place. The quiet last day of our European trip.

Donald B. Gibson

DEPARTURE

MONDAY, SEPTEMBER 4

I was the first one awake. As always I carefully considered the possible hindrances to our our well laid plans: fire, tornado, earthquake, flood.

We went to breakfast. I had tea only and not much of that. We returned, packed, and left the Y.W.C. A. for the British Airways Coach Station and Heathrow Airport.

At British Airways they could not check our bags in because Air India was having difficulty of some kind and there was talk of passengers being shifted to another flight. When we got to Heathrow, we checked in, only to be told to return in an hour or so to see what our status was.

Well, it all finally worked out--not quickly--not easily, but it did. We are now over the Atlantic and when I write again, I'm going to sum it up, tell you what the meaning of the trip has all been. If nothing follows so far, if you don't have an update, it's because I haven't put it all down yet. But hold on!! There's still time ...

POSTLUDE

FORTY YEARS LATER

After the promise made to myself all those many years ago, I have finally returned to my journal and to that special time with my boys. Typing it up has been like taking the journey again. It was a wonderful time despite the challenges and it has been wonderful to relive it.

I have given myself access not only to a very special trip but also to the childhoods of my now adult sons. I look forward to sharing these memories with them.

Donald B. Gibson

97101012R00042

Made in the USA
Lexington, KY
26 August 2018